WRITING
UKRAINE

MYRNA KOSTASH

WRITING UKRAINE

AU PRESS

"TO INVESTIGATE, REVEAL, AND PASS JUDGEMENT," the writer, publisher, and critic, George Melnyk, wrote in appreciation of *All of Baba's Children*. This is a fair summary of my procedures as a nonfiction writer of the School of New Journalism who lived for three months in the summer of 1975 in the Frontenac Motel in Two Hills Alberta (in the Ukrainian bloc settlement NE of Edmonton) and made the rounds of the community with a Sony cassette tape recorder and notebook.

I did interviews with many questions, I read secondary sources, and even dived into original sources stashed away in boxes in basements—minutes of school district meetings, Christmas Concert programs, and issues of the *Vegreville Observer* from the 1930s—and I passed judgement on it all. Rereading *All of Baba's Children* forty-five years later, I find it brashly confident and overwrought in places where I held forth on the history of Ukraine, on the Ukrainian Orthodox Church, and on the class stratification of Canadian society whose "mainstream" I insisted on calling Anglo-Saxon throughout. I had been away from Alberta and the Edmonton Ukrainian Canadian community for ten years but wrote with all the authority of the New Journalist: reporting with a Great Big Fat Attitude.

An exploration of Ukrainian Canadian identity in the 1970s: why *Baba's Children*? As a non-Anglo female nonfiction writer from the prairies, I thought of myself as an outsider to the Canadian mainstream, an assertion I make repeatedly in the book as a kind of heartbeat, bent on understanding the "otherness" that lay in my roots in Ukrainian settlement in Alberta and in its culture if not values. This was not a particularly introspective project. Although I was interested in ethnicity as an identity marker, I rarely referred to my own experience of this ethnic otherness. While still writing *All of Baba's Children*, I wrote a piece for *Saturday Night* magazine that the editor titled "Baba Was a Bohunk." In fact, I announced myself as a white, middle-class Anglophone with a weak attachment to the Ukrainian Canadian community in which I had grown up in Edmonton. But I did identify as a feminist, a New Journalist, an alumna of 1960s politics and rock 'n roll. And so themes that emerged from my interviews in Two Hills—the ruling class's exploitation of Ukrainian Canadian workers, the compulsion of Anglicization, rural poverty (especially among women), racism toward "bohunks"—these were all grist for my mill as I investigated,

I THOUGHT OF MYSELF AS AN OUTSIDER TO THE CANADIAN MAINSTREAM, AN ASSERTION I MAKE REPEATEDLY IN THE BOOK AS A KIND OF HEARTBEAT

revealed, and passed judgement on the story of the first generation of Ukrainian Canadians born in Canada (my parents' generation). By the time I had finished writing the book (it was published in 1978), I declared that "I felt at home in Two Hills." So much so that I bought a quarter section with a log shack six miles north of town, acquired a Co-op membership card, and had mail rerouted to General Delivery for the summers.

I was the second generation born in Canada of Ukrainian forebears and was fully aware of my generation's responsibility to contest the work of the earlier intelligentsia. These were the writers, community activists, teachers, priests, lawyers, and local politicians whom I excoriated as propagandists of the ethnic cliché, the "hackneyed version of the Canadian myth of happiness." It was my responsibility to call them out on what was manifestly untrue about this myth, what was unspoken or evaded or belittled. And so I decried the absence of accounts of Ukrainian Canadian *unhappiness* and failure—rural poverty, male domestic violence, illiteracy, premature deaths, labour abuses, racist stereotyping, shame—a veritable threnody of miserabilism.

I quote an interviewee: "My parents had another girl but that girl died, small. My father was killed by a train crossing a track in Vegreville. Brother Bill died, sick with something, some infection in his foot. Whatever he had, we don't know, but he died. There were no doctors."

These were the darker corners of Ukrainian Canadian identity to which I added a miserabilism of my own, describing them as "this mass of poor and thwarted people."

OLD HOUSE IN DZHURIV, 1984.

I was however feeling something more than just rage against the machinery of Anglo-Canadian capitalist assimilationist ruling class dominance. That much was my intellectual swagger, but I had another itinerary in and around Two Hills. I was invited to weddings; I volunteered to sell hot dogs at the rodeo; with my father I dropped in on the Orthodox priest and his wife for tea; I drank beer in the hotel bar in Hairy Hill; roamed around country cemeteries and admired the luxuriant gardens as I strolled down alleyways. I went to see Ukrainian dancers in Vegreville and bought an old milk can at a farm auction. And all the time I was listening.

I sat in the cafe of the Two Hills Hotel, scribbling innocently in a notebook while keeping my ears tuned to conversation in the next booth, whether about fertilizer or date squares recipes. All of it was fascinating to a city girl. I wandered into the hall and joined a circle of women, their nylon stockings rolled down to their ankles in the heat, taking my turn in rolling rice into cabbage leaves: there would be a wedding later that day. Two couples who played bridge together invited me to their reminiscences while passing the bottle of rye around, a bowl of ice cubes and the bottle of Coke. I heard the story of how, when everyone still lived on the farms, platforms were set up in the granary as a dancing floor and when it got dark kerosene lanterns were hung on nails in rafters so that the orchestra could keep on playing until dawn.

Retrospectively, I see that the Ukrainian Canadian culture I was immersed in was almost exclusively rural and for all its accommodations to Canadian "progress" was redolent of Old Country nostalgia and Canadian sentimentality, "a little bit of this, a little bit of that": a Byzantine icon and a calendar picture of a blonde Miss Alberta Wheat Pool cuddling chicks; a cross-stitched cushion cover and a chocolate Easter bunny; pyrohy in the saucepan and a can of Empress strawberry jam on the pantry shelf. In the national hall, the stage curtains were decorated with idyllic scenes of life in the Galician village c. 1900: the thatched-roof cottage, the giant sunflowers and red poppies in the yard, the gooseherd flirting with the maid at the gate.

I wrote a little harshly about the Ukrainian Canadian reproduction of the idealized village they had never visited but at the same time I acknowledged that here were instances of the struggle for dignity and self-respect among a disregarded cultural minority in Canada. As I pointed out, "demonstrably few others outside the community are concerned about the two-fold threat to Ukrainian identity from Russification in the old country and Americanization in the new."

But I was uneasy all the same and recovered my swagger as an "outsider," even to my own community's sense of achievement. "The ruling class isn't likely to shake in its boots," I observed at the sight of a Ukrainian Canadian MLA wearing an embroidered shirt under his suit jacket in the Legislature. "The act of speaking Ukrainian four generations after immigration will not bring back to life the whole communities subsumed within Anglo-American technological civilization." And so I concluded, in the last lines of *All of Baba's Children,* "a tourist I came, a tourist I leave," and returned to the Anglo-American metropolis, Edmonton, away from ethnic sideroads. The metropolis, after all, is where Baba meant to have me live.

Well, that was then, this is now. "Now" is when I review a text written almost half a century ago and make a few salient observations about that younger writer.

The first is that I was still writing in the style and voice of what I call full-tilt-boogie nonfiction rather characteristic of the magazine journalism I had already practised as a freelancer in Toronto. Thus the sometimes-overwrought vocabulary of a political evangelist: frequent references to the "Canadian capitalist ruling class" or to the "spilled blood" of the strikers in Estevan, Saskatchewan, that "fertilized the militant consciousness of

Ukrainian Canadians"—and an obsessive reduction of the Canadian bourgeoisie to "Anglo-Saxons." I would write only one more book in that voice.

The second observation is the very shadowy presence of Indigenous people, whether in my interviewees' narratives or in my own. Indigenous neighbours are never mentioned but "Indian trails" and disadvantaged Métis from northern Alberta are, as well as the attitude of social supremacy of the Ukrainian Canadian woman who "feels sorry for Indians because they are so backward." I wrote of the "incarceration of native people on reservations [sic]" but never mention how they came to be there—no mention of Treaty Six or the Homestead Act. (It must be said that none of my many reviewers in 1979, including the hostile ones, mentioned these lacunae either.)

BUT I WAS UNEASY ALL THE SAME AND RECOVERED MY SWAGGER AS AN "OUTSIDER," EVEN TO MY OWN COMMUNITY'S SENSE OF ACHIEVEMENT

The third observation: In 1975, in the Ukrainian Canadian bloc settlement, where and what was Ukraine? Unapologetically, I took the position that I was a (hyphenated) Ukrainian Canadian and that actually existing Ukraine (a *Soviet Socialist Republic*, let us recall) had no purchase on my identity. I was severely

judgemental about those in the community I called "nationalists," that is, right-wing anti-Communists who voted Social
Credit and sent their kids to summer camp to march around in
uniforms and commit themselves to the liberation of Ukraine
by any means necessary. My sympathies lay elsewhere, with
the "progressive" Ukrainian Canadians of Two Hills who had
been part of farmers' strikes during the Depression and voted
CCF (Co-operative Commonwealth Federation), never went to
church, favouring membership in the ULFTA (Ukrainian Labour
Farmer Temple Association) in whose plain halls down a rural
road they congregated for mandolin concerts and amateur pro-
ductions of recent Soviet Ukrainian plays.

However, in rereading *All of Baba's Children*, I now take note
of how often events recounted and arguments substantiated and
my reaction to them are a kind of stand-in for Ukraine both as
Old Country lost in the mists of nostalgia and as a geopolitical
reality that one was either "for" or "against."

I wrote swaths of potted Ukrainian history and depended
on a couple of recent scholarly tomes to expose the catastrophe
that was Galician land poverty and social oppression at the turn
of the twentieth century. Turning to an account of the nationally
awakened intelligentsia in Galicia, I wrote of how students and

teachers had helped organize the reading societies [*chytal'ni*] in Galician villages that inspired the Ukrainian Canadian national hall [*narodnyi dim*] about which many of my interviewees spoke in gratitude for the cultural activities that were organized there. Other enlightened Galicians organized social democratic political parties and proto-feminist societies, versions of which made their way to western Canada. (It should be recalled that Galicia—now part of western Ukraine—was in 1900 and until 1918 a province of the Austro-Hungarian Empire and elected social democrats to the parliament in Vienna.)

But it seemed to me that all this functioned as a kind of ancestral memory. It wasn't until the new Canadian-educated intelligentsia emerged, as teachers, newspaper editors, doctors, lawyers, left-wing as well as right-wing, that actually existing Soviet Ukraine, the contested homeland, the motherland, came into view of the community in Canada.

This was Ukraine, a constituent part of the USSR, a workers' state, or prison, depending on your politics, that represented to some of my interviewees who had led a "hard, bitter life" in Canada a chance, through Communism, at "vengeance, of revenge against the ruling class." For their part, anti-Communists denounced policies of the Soviet Union that were crushing the dissident intellectuals and artists of the oppressed Ukrainian nation. But also, rising in the 1960s and 1970s, yet another noisy group of Ukrainian Canadians had arrived, ones who paraded with placards and banners in front of Soviet consulates: *Free Valentyn Moroz! Down with the bogus show trials!*

Who, I wondered, was Valentyn Moroz?

And then I went to Ukraine.

Having read *All of Baba's Children* my readers would often ask, "So, when are you going back to Ukraine?" (This was a common locution: going back to a place you'd never been.) I had no intention of going. I was a deeply rooted Canadian, caught up in the discovery of a community of like-minded Ukrainian Edmontonians. But in 1984 I did go, and again in 1988, and the partial fruit of those two trips was my 1993 book, *Bloodlines: A Journey into Eastern Europe.*

I did not take a tape recorder—instead, I scribbled notes in amateurish code of conversations, all clandestine—and waited until I had crossed over the border to Poland to write my notes as fully as memory, still fresh, served. Post-Solidarity Poland, so recently shaken by strikes, riots and civil disobedience and the imposition of martial law, was immeasurably a more open society than the Ukrainian SSR. Or so it felt to me: "I could breathe

WOMEN'S MEETING IN WARSAW, POLAND, 1987.

again," I noted. Crossing the border from Poland to Communist Czechoslovakia, truly a police state, meant choking again with every breath.

In fact, Ukraine was a side-trip from the main itinerary, Eastern Europe—several trips I made from the mid- to late 1980s through Yugoslavia, Czechoslovakia, and Poland, before the fall of the Berlin Wall in 1989 and the complete reordering of the geopolitical map.

Inspired by the work I had done for my second book, *Long Way from Home: The Story of the Sixties Generation in Canada*, I turned my attention to the Generation of 1968 in places like Warsaw, Prague, Belgrade, and Zagreb, sites of youthful rebellious contestation against the oppressive apparatus of authoritarian regimes. There had been no "1968" in Ukraine but as I was to learn there had been the Sixties People [*Shistdesiatnyky*], some of whom I would meet in Kyiv and Lviv.

But, first, Ukraine was the village.

In 1984, when western visitors were still prohibited from visiting relatives in villages in western Ukraine, the village was Dzhuriv, birthplace of my maternal grandparents. The next generations laboured on collective farms and, after 1962, kept up a correspondence of sorts with my mother and aunt who, in

THE AUTHOR (SEATED, SECOND FROM LEFT) WITH FAMILY IN UKRAINE, 1984.

return, sent the fabled *banderoli*, boxes filled with used clothes. My second cousins contrived to have me spend a day with them regardless and so I, granddaughter of their beloved Palahna, my Baba, who had left in 1911 and never came back, was welcomed in her stead. The emotional impact of that reunion was caught in a photograph in which old Katrusia, matriarch of the extended family, holds out to me the traditional and ceremonial gifts of welcome: a braided bread and a thimble of salt [*khlib i sil'*] on an embroidered cloth [*rushnyk*] draping her hands. I receive it, and looking into the camera, I weep.

This moment was the emotional culmination of my encounter with the village, a real one in real Ukraine. It was distantly related to the one depicted on so many Ukrainian Canadian stage curtains and calendars and song sheets but here was the actually existing Ukrainian *selo*, set in the rolling contours of farmland, the fields (collective farms, I eventually acknowledged) laid out in large splotches and not in the grid of the Canadian quarter-sections. I thought how dismal Alberta must have looked—bush and slough and scrawny aspen—compared to this lush greenery (it was June). But I could also see there was another village, Katrusia's house for instance, with no hot running water or indoor plumbing, and the single paved street,

DMYTRO AND KATRUSIA (MIDDLE, RIGHT) PRESENTING THE AUTHOR
WITH A BRAIDED BREAD AND A THIMBLE OF SALT [*KHLIB I SIL'*]
ON AN EMBROIDERED CLOTH [*RUSHNYK*]. DZHURIV, 1984.

and abandoned cottages, much like their counterparts on the Canadian prairie, subsiding under the weight of their mouldering thatched roofs into a yard gone wild with grasses and yellow daisies. It would not be the first time that I wondered: what happened to the Revolution?

My own maternal grandfather, Dido Andrew, subproletarian ditch-digger in Edmonton, never abandoned his youthful admiration of the achievements of the 1917 Bolshevik Revolution (that spread out with great violence at the point of Red Army bayonets to east and central Ukraine): land redistribution, rural mechanization (tractors!), all kids to school, everyone to the exuberant May Day parades, and most impressive of all, the Fatherland's great victory over the German occupying army (On to Berlin!). Dictatorship of the Proletariat had delivered this cornucopia of happiness to the very class of men and women so despised and ground down by the Capitalist Bosses of Edmonton.

But in Kyiv in 1984 I was in a constant rage. I cannot say I came unprepared; an upbringing in the Ukrainian Canadian community during the Cold War had impressed upon me the catastrophe that Soviet Communism had been for the Ukrainian people. But here it was in its shabby reality, in the lives of individuals, the ones who shuffled about in ill-fitting jeans and appalling footwear, carrying shopping bags in the ever-hopeful expectation of coming across something rare and wonderful in the shops: New cucumbers? Baby clothes? A volume of Ukrainian poetry? The livid exhaustion on women's faces as they stood patiently in queues like mendicants in line-ups at the bins of turnips and onions. The land is broad and generous: why were people lining up for bad food? I noticed the slatternly service in the fast-food cafes, workers quickly chewing the shreds of salad, bits of herring, watery bowls of pyrohy, faces close to their bowls as if they have only recently begun to eat their fill.

IT WOULD NOT BE THE FIRST TIME THAT I WONDERED: WHAT HAPPENED TO THE REVOLUTION?

And everywhere, it felt, I was made aware of the cry, *Говорите по-человечески! Govoritie po-chieloviechieski!* Speak human! By human they of course meant Russian. Downtown Kyiv: a battered delivery truck canters through the intersection, bearing the utilitarian logo, *Khlieb*. Russian for bread. In Ukraine, legendary breadbasket, mythologized as the Earth Mother cradling a sheaf of wheat in her round, stout arms— there are public statues like this everywhere—they eat bread in Russian. It reminded me of Québécois Michelle Lalonde's iconic 1968 poem "Speak White!" She is angry, aggressive, even bitter, as she condemns the linguistic, cultural, and economic exploitation and oppression of the Québécois by the suffocating dominance of English language and Anglo-American culture.

And I remember the American reporter who, in 2022, recoiled from the "jarring" militaristic praise by Ukrainians for the heroism of their Ukrainian forces in defence of the violated homeland against Russian invasion.

Jarring. And was my righteous anger in *All of Baba's Children* "jarring" when I railed against the humiliation of the Ukrainian Canadian "bohunks" by the Anglophone elites?

Finally, in Odesa, last stop on the prescribed itinerary, I met by chance Seriozha, a Soviet Ukrainian drop-out. That is how I was thinking of him as he raised a toast in the flat of his friend, a squatter, to the Polish workers' movement, Solidarity, by then outlawed in Poland. "Good for them! They go on strike. They don't work. More power to them." He refuses to pay the fare on the tram, arguing that one of the Resolutions of the Twenty-Fourth Party Congress had promised free public transport by 1970; it's already 1984. He shares a two-room flat with his mother, a survivor of the engineered famine, Holodomor, in the 1930s.

She's asleep as he tiptoes around to make a mug of tea and slice up some withered torte. I look around at the things on his walls: a crucifix, a photograph of John Lennon, a calendar. He leaps up. He has two treasures to show, he says. He lifts up the calendar. Taped to the wall behind it hangs the doleful visage of Alexander Solzhenitsyn, former Gulag inmate now in exile in the US, author of the monumental *Gulag Archipelago*. He walks to his bed and pulls out from under the mattress a novel by Stephen King.

I feared for him. Had I been followed to his flat? Would he be visited the next day by state authorities and threatened with . . . well, what? Eviction, out on the street with his mother, his treasures seized as evidence of anti-Soviet propaganda, and he hustled off to a hard labour camp? I had been so rattled by the pervading sense of having been watched that I waited until I was in Poland to write up the notes of my entire Ukrainian visit.

As my visit with the relatives in Dzhuriv wound down, I was led to a modest war monument at the top of the main road. I sensed that I was meant to read the inscribed scroll of names, and indeed there was the name of my Baba's brother, Yuri Kosovan, for whom she had ceaselessly mourned in Canada, included among several others: "These perished at the hands of Ukrainian Bourgeois Nationalists [anti-Soviet guerrilla army resisting Soviet occupation of western Ukraine at the end of World War ii], with gratitude from the workers of the village of Dzhuriv." I took a photograph. There was no conversation. I would not revisit this quiet moment, and its import to the meaning of "family history," until I sat down to write *Ghosts in a Photograph* thirty years later.

1988: my second trip to Ukraine took place in a profoundly altered context. The entire ussr was in the throes of *perestroika* [rebuilding] and *glasnost* [openness]—*perebudova* and *hlasnist* in Ukrainian—a campaign driven from the top by general secretary of the Communist Party, Mikhail Gorbachev. I bought a poster: "Citizen! What have *you* done for perestroika?" Second cousin Pavlina came to Kyiv to spend a couple of days with me. In the interval since we had last visited in the village, I had learned to speak Ukrainian and she had learned to speak "glasnost."

While a bottle of *shampanskoie* lay cooling in the toilet bowl of my hotel room, Pavlina held forth on: the Holodomor, Leon Trotsky, founder of the Red Army, the horrors of collectivization—I signalled to be wary of the bugs in the room but she waved this away, "Don't be crazy"—purges of Ukrainian intellectuals, purges of army officers just before the Nazi invasion of Soviet Ukraine . . . Her exposés were fiery, evangelical, and I responded gently: "I know all this, Pavlina, but how do *you* know it?" Soviet journalism had bloomed in the new reality of openness—"I read *our* newspapers"— and I realized that there was likewise a pivot in her relationship with a relative from Canada. Pavlina had no need of a Ukrainian Canadian second cousin to tell her the news sotto voce as a kind of contraband. No need of my sympathy or pity for her Communist-engineered ignorance.

EVEN IN THE PAGES OF AN INKY PROVINCIAL BROADSHEET A SOOTY SMUDGE OF CHEAP PRINTER'S INK COULD FILL IN A BLANK

With every page of a newspaper or magazine she was growing smarter. Even in the pages of an inky provincial broadsheet a sooty smudge of cheap printer's ink could fill in a blank.

1988 Kyiv: Ukraine was marking the 1,000th anniversary of the Baptism of Rus into Christianity via Byzantium, and perestroika had allowed for a certain revival of public religious devotions.[1] I joined the multitude who had crowded into St Volodymyr's Orthodox Cathedral for the Divine Liturgy, or at least to witness the spectacle. An hour into the Mass, as I felt the full-throated rumble of the familiar responses (*Lord have mercy, Lord have mercy, Lord have mercy*), the yearning melancholy of the hymns and the communal devotions of the crowd, many in from the villages and collective farms, I stood in awe of the collective memory intact across a thousand years of violated memory—Mongols, Tatars, Poles and Czars and Bolsheviks, war, terror, famine, occupations, Gulag, silence, and fear—and in awe that they remember how to do this, be faithful to their place in the genealogy of baptized Rus. If I reflect again on this it is because it foreshadows a book I would publish twenty-two years later, *Prodigal Daughter: A Journey to Byzantium*.

In its way, this prayerful multitude was speaking a truth to power in concert with the activists in Ukrainian intellectual and cultural circles who had recently come up from the underground and out of the shadows, and home from the Gulag. I knew of them as the *Shistdesiatnyky*. Their raised Ukrainian national consciousness in the early 1960s and later in the 1970s led to creative outbursts in literature, theatre, film, journalism, and

---

1   The Rus founded the first consolidated state among the eastern Slavs, centred on Kyiv.

NUNS IN A PROCESSION TO MARK THE 1,000 ANNIVERSARY
OF RUSSIAN CHRISTIANITY. KYIV, 1988.

art; and when that had all been brutally quashed by show trials and prison, they engaged in human rights protests and clandestine cultural production.

In 1988 I was taken around to the earlier sites of their activism—a cinema, an auditorium, a park monument—and to an interview with Halyna Sevruk, a ceramic artist long expelled from the Union of Artists of Ukraine for protesting the mass arrests of writers and artists—and to a string of stories about the murdered artist Alla Horska (she had designed a "nationalist" stained glass window of Ukraine's national poet Taras Shevchenko, 1814–1861) and the fate of the dissident poet Vasyl Stus, dead in the Gulag in 1985, repeatedly rearrested for activism in human rights groups. (In 1997 I published a memoir, *The Doomed Bridegroom,* in which his story comprises a chapter.)

As heroic and exciting as the stories were that I had been learning from underground activists in Eastern Europe, nothing had prepared me for the dogged resistance unto death of the Ukrainian artists and intellectuals of the 1960s and 1970s, returning again and again to the scenes of their "crimes," whether rising to shout in a cinema or circulating samizdat (*samvydav* in Ukrainian) or standing sentinel outside a courtroom or reciting a banned poem at the lip of a friend's grave.

HALYNA SEVRUK, A CERAMIC ARTIST WHO WAS EXPELLED FROM
THE UNION OF ARTISTS OF UKRAINE FOR PROTESTING THE MASS
ARRESTS OF WRITERS AND ARTISTS. KYIV, 1988.

For a Ukrainian Canadian—like it or not, resistance is futile—Ukraine is not a country like other countries. Everything about it is loaded, freighted with meaning. Kyiv is not just a capital city, it is the motherlode of Rus. The Dnipro is not just a major water artery bifurcating Ukraine, it is the fertilizing waters of Cossack military settlement and anti-imperial campaigns. Folk songs at weddings in Soviet Ukrainian restaurants are subversive manifestations of the unquenchable spirit of the *narod*, the people. The verdant, rolling countryside of my grandparents' home villages is a boneyard of the victims of peasant wars, occupations, genocidal famines, pogroms. For the visiting Ukrainian Canadian such as myself, I was reminded at every turn that Ukraine is not merely *interesting*; its entire environment is a disclosure of the subversive meaning of Ukrainian history.

Growing up in Edmonton, this had often made me squirm— the Ukrainian language was not just a form of speech but the genetic memory of an imperilled nation and who was I to study French and Russian instead? But now in 1988 this had become clear: I could draw a line from the exploited, defiant masses of Ukrainian Canadians I had stood in solidarity with (which is how I came to understand what my project was in *All of Baba's Children*) to the poets of Ukraine through whom Ukraine had managed to remember itself.

There was still a village to visit, that of my paternal grand-parents; and this being perestroika, I was offered a car and chauffeur by the Union of Ukrainian Writers to make the trip to Tulova. My visit unfolded sweetly as once again I made the rounds of a circle of relations whose existence I had been quite unaware of, but who carry the oral memory of Anna and Fedir Kostashchuk who left Tulova in 1900. I later discovered, back in Edmonton, that there had also been a sustained correspondence between my father and one of his cousins in Tulova, about which he had never spoken to me. (I found the letters after his death.) Their arrival onto their homestead in Alberta is the foundational story of their descendants in Canada and I was ignorant of the stories of the Kostashchuks who never left Galicia, including the one buried in the village cemetery, Vasyl Kostashchuk, a writer (1896–1973). Writer. *Writer.* Utterly unknown to us Kostashes variously BED, MEd, BA, MA, MSC, in Canada. Yet, back in Kyiv, I was presented a well-thumbed copy of Vasyl Kostashchuk's book and an account of its considerable value to a young poet, a *Shistdesiatnyk,* of Galicia.

THE UKRAINIAN LANGUAGE WAS NOT JUST A FORM OF SPEECH BUT THE GENETIC MEMORY OF AN IMPERILLED NATION

An account of the last time I was in Ukraine, in 2013, is folded into my new book, *Ghosts in a Photograph*, where it informs chapters about relatives on both sides of my family whose life stories in Ukraine were, at best, vaguely accounted for; at worst, simply unknown. They elicited in me the question "Who?" that set me on a spree of what I think of as sleuthing, but as much narratives of fortuitous happenstance as of following trails of clues laid down unwittingly, waiting for a long-lost Canadian relative to sniff them out.

And so, through these stories and their contexts I came to know some specifics of Ukrainian history I hadn't known I was interested in or, interested, didn't know where to look. These were, partially: peasant and workers' strikes in Galicia in the 1920s; the history of the suppressed Communist Party of Western Ukraine; the disillusionment of a young writer, a social democrat in Soviet-occupied Kyiv in the 1930s; the brutality unleashed by the Soviet occupation of western Ukraine 1939–1941; the extermination of the Jews of Kolomyia in Galicia; the horrors of Nazi occupation across the whole of Ukraine 1941–1944; the literary biography of a teacher-writer in Tulova in the Ukrainian SSR 1896–1975; how Soviet power was reimposed in western Ukraine after 1945; the ultimately futile but bitter and ferocious guerrilla war to drive the occupiers out 1945–1953 in which some Kostashchuks of Tulova had enlisted.

If this partial listing of catastrophes and their consequences brings to mind current geopolitical events, that is as it should be, given Ukraine's agonies during the war of brutal aggression and massive criminality that was launched definitively in February 2022 by Russia against Ukraine's territorial sovereignty and biological survival. I had finished writing *Ghosts in a Photograph* well before the war began but I expect the book's readers will have it back of mind while reading certain of its chapters in which I reconstruct the circumstances of my Ukrainian relatives' lives from 1939 to 1951.

But *Ghosts* is also and primarily a series of profiles of my five grandparents whose lives began in Galician villages and ended in Edmonton or on farms east of Edmonton near Vegreville. After a long detour away from *All of Baba's Children*, I was interested in the lives of these forebears as viewed, 120 years after their immigration to Alberta, through the lens of my own life experiences. And so, in striking contrast to my evangelical voice and stance in *All of Baba's Children*, in *Ghosts in a Photograph* I am fully present at the events described (as good a definition as any of what literary or creative nonfiction does): alive to my own emotions and excavated memories, often regretting that I was writing too late to have my curiosity and perplexity satisfied.

I also return, wiser and humbler, to some of the material in *All of Baba's Children*. I'm thinking of how I now understand a grandfather's pro-Soviet sympathies; the everyday labours of an illiterate woman on a homestead, in the case of a grandmother; the details of Ukrainian Canadian cultural life in Edmonton, especially the theatre, in the case of another grandmother; the loneliness of the educated *gimnasia* [high school] graduate as he bent to the task of building a thatched-roof *khata* in the Alberta parkland bush, in the case of another grandfather.

Ghosts in a Photograph concludes in a coda: "On the Land." I have earlier referred to the "very shadowy presence of Indigenous people" in *All of Baba's Children*. But, decades later, a gravesite off the beaten track near Fort Battleford in Saskatchewan—in fact the mass grave of eight Indigenous warriors who had been hanged together, in November 1885—proved an emotional and intellectual turning point, even a reckoning, for me as the granddaughter of settlers. In Canada's only mass hanging, the warriors had been condemned for the slayings of nine unarmed men at Frog Lake settlement earlier that year. I knew nothing about it, and so I stood transfixed at the granite stone.

AUTHOR AT THE WANDERING SPIRIT MASS GRAVE IN
FORT BATTLEFORD, SASKATCHEWAN.

Up to that moment, I had not taken note of how narrow was the slit in time between the two events: the crushing in 1885 of the last resistance in Canada's North-West to incarceration on the reserves, and the arrival in June 1900 of my paternal grandparents en route to their promised land, 160 acres of homestead in the parkland bush. Fifteen years. The gap was fifteen years— but it may as well have been an eon between two chronologies, as though all that had gone before "our" arrival and possession of the land belonged to unrecorded time.

In *Ghosts in a Photograph* I put those dates in relationship. In fact there is an earlier date, 1876, the signing of Treaty Six at Fort Carlton, and I am its beneficiary. For, exactly one hundred years later, on 30 September 1976, the Land Titles office of North Alberta Land Registration District certified that Myrna Ann Kostash "is now the owner of an estate," the NE Quarter of Section 31 in Township 55 at Range 12, w of the 4th Meridian—almost six miles due north of the town of Two Hills—"containing 160 acres, more or less." It had a livable shack with wood-burning stove, an outhouse, and a rain barrel, and so I moved in for the summers. By the time *All of Baba's Children* was published in January 1978, I had a name for my estate: I named it after the ancestral village of the Kostashes, and I nailed a rustic board to the outside wall by the door, inscribed in white paint: TULOVA.

To me, the name echoed the western-most point of my forebears' journey to Canada. By nailing up the board painted with the letters TULOVA, I was laying claim, two generations later, to the memory of leave-taking, uprooting, and exodus. But I was also announcing that that exodus had a terminus: it came to an end, a "somewhere," a "here," which, two generations later, would symbolically terminate in the location I called home. Forty-five years on, I can now appreciate what I had unknowingly done: brought into a single imagined space the two historical sources of my identity: a homestead on Treaty Six Territory and a village in Galicia circa 1900.

In 2003 and 2004, I made several road trips to towns and historic sites along the North Saskatchewan River. As I took the measure of its course from the Rockies to Lake Winnipeg, I was also taking measure of the history (primordial, ecological, human, cultural) associated with this waterway. This is how the stories of bison hunts and geological surveys, of the fur trade and Christian missions and North-West Mounted Police posts, of piles of bleaching bison bones, of Treaties, of the Indian Act and the CPR, and of the 1885 Northwest Resistance seeped into my western Canadian consciousness and conscience until they were drenched to the roots.

There was the stark and brute reality of Cree hunger and of the smallpox that ravaged them in the early 1870s interpreted through the language of appeal for famine relief and medicines. What was wanted was guarantees that the Crown would provide for the basic security of people who could see what was coming.

And so we "white men" arrived by steamship and railway, thousands of us, and spread ourselves across the ceded territory now laid out in an implacable grid of homesteads and we settled in, we settled down. We had been shoeless peasants in the Old Country; here in the new we were farmers, and well-shod. For such bounty we had the Canadian government and Queen Victoria to thank. Cree chiefs had signed off on Treaty Six: what had this to do with us?

The Canadian Encyclopedia is succinct: From the Crown's point of view, treaties provided the legal surrender of Indigenous Rights to the land. From the Indigenous point of view, even as they were signing, treaties provided for "relationships between autonomous peoples who agree to share the lands and resources of Canada. Seen from the Indigenous perspective, treaties do not surrender rights; rather, they confirm Indigenous rights."[2]

2 The Canadian Encyclopedia, "Treaties with Indigenous Peoples in Canada," *The Canadian Encyclopedia*, 6 June 2011, Last Edited September 11, 2017, https://www.thecanadianencyclopedia.ca/en/article/aboriginal-treaties.

Agree. Share. Rights. Relationships.

I turned to my friend the Edmonton poet Naomi McIlwraith who writes in her "second / Mother tongue," Cree, as well as in English. She writes: "Listen. Can you hear the lyricism in the language / of *nêhiyawak*?" We met in a neighbourhood shawarma diner. She scribbled on a piece of paper and turned the words to me:

Older brother: *ostêsimâw*
Something written: *masinahikan*
Treaty: *ostêsimâwasinahikan*
Treaty: a relationship with brothers, written and signed

Relationship, says Naomi, is kinship, understood as much more than blood; it is an alliance. We have been delivered an invitation.

What does "Ukraine" mean to the sixth (and counting) generation in Canada? And now counting the newcomers who have fled war in Ukraine and settled in Edmonton? They are a vital replenishment of the cultural gene pool: if they were to visit Two Hills in 2024, for instance, they would find it a settlement of Mennonite farmers from Mexico with virtually all traces of an earlier community of Ukrainian Canadians erased, blown over by the dust and chaff that now swirls off their fields as vast and featureless as a Soviet *kolhosp* (collective farm). The Ukrainian Canadians have moved on, some who I had interviewed fifty years ago now lying in the municipal cemetery. But there is a museum, the Ukrainian Cultural Heritage Village, on Highway 16, the gateway to the historic Ukrainian bloc settlement country further east. If you never had relatives who you visited on a farm near Myrnam or had seen a live chicken or if you were born long after the totemic wooden grain elevator was demolished as the last rail spur line was torn up or had no idea you could extract oil from coal, this is an excellent place to learn something of a history now more than 125-years-old. *Something* of a history. . . . When I put the word "Treaty" into the Ukrainian Cultural Village's website search engine, I was informed: "Your Search yielded no results."[3] But keep browsing the site and you will find a dandy recipe for *borshch*.

3   "Ukrainian Cultural Heritage Village," accessed 13 February 2024, https://ukrainianvillage.ca/

DZHURIV VILLAGER IN HER GARDEN, 1984.

Born and raised in Edmonton, **MYRNA KOSTASH** arrived on the literary scene in 1977 with the publication of the now classic *All of Baba's Children*. She is the author, among many other titles, of *Bloodlines: A Journey into Eastern Europe* (1993), which won the Alberta Culture and Writers' Guild of Alberta prize for Best Non-Fiction, *The Doomed Bridegroom: A Memoir* (1998), and *Prodigal Daughter: A Journey to Byzantium* (2010), which received the 2011 City of Edmonton Book Prize and the 2011 Writers' Guild of Alberta Wilfred Eggleston Award for Best Nonfiction. Her most recent publication, *Ghosts in a Photograph: A Chronicle*, was honoured with the Shevchenko Foundation's 2024 Kobzar Book Award. Kostash, who has served as president of the Writers' Guild of Alberta and as chair of the Writers' Union of Canada, has lectured all across Canada and in Europe on a wide array of contemporary topics. In 2010, she was awarded the Writers' Trust of Canada's Matt Cohen Award: In Celebration of a Writing Life.

Library and Archives Canada Cataloguing in Publication
Title: Writing Ukraine / Myrna Kostash.
Names: Kostash, Myrna, author.
Identifiers: Canadiana (print) 20240351878 | Canadiana (ebook) 20240351894
 | ISBN 9781771994224 (softcover) | ISBN 9781771994248 (EPUB) | ISBN
 9781771994231 (PDF)
Subjects: LCSH: Ukrainians—Canada—Ethnic identity. | LCSH: Russian Invasion
 of Ukraine, 2022—Influence. | CSH: Ukrainian Canadians—Ethnic identity.
Classification: LCC FC106.U5 K684 2024 | DDC 971/.00491791—dc23

We acknowledge the financial support of the Government of Canada through
the Canada Book Fund (CBF) for our publishing activities and the assistance
provided by the Government of Alberta through the Alberta Media Fund.